EXPLORING
Historic Hilo

NASH

EXPLORING
Historic Hilo

Leslie Lang

Watermark Publishing

Second Printing

ISBN-10 0-9779143-6-4
ISBN-13 978-0-9779143-6-4

Library of Congress Control Number: 2006935633

Design
Leo Gonzalez

Production
Maggie Fujino

Exploring Historic Hilo is an ongoing community effort. Readers with additional information about any of the photos or captions in this book are invited to contact the publisher at the mailing address or email address below.

Watermark Publishing
1088 Bishop Street, Suite 310
Honolulu, HI 96813
Telephone: Toll-free 1-866-900-BOOK
Web site: www.bookshawaii.net
email: sales@watermark.net

Printed in the United States

Contents

Acknowledgments

Gathering old photos and their stories for this book has been like stepping back into gracious old Hilo itself. So many people have generously shared their memories and stories about old Hilo, many inviting the author into their homes where they pulled photos off the wall and opened fading photo albums. This book wouldn't exist without the generosity of friends old and new.

Mahalo a nui loa to Curtis Narimatsu, whose knowledge of historic Hilo and generosity in sharing his research are truly remarkable; to Erling Hedemann, Jr., for very kindly sharing his grandfather's incredible photo collection; to Ian Birnie, whose knowledge of Hilo's railroad past is extensive, and whose generous help, the same; and to the late Kent Warshauer, the *Hawaii Tribune-Herald*'s "Sugar Spy," whose "Riddle of the Relic" articles have long been, and will continue to be, a fabulous and highly appreciated resource.

Sincere thanks, as well, to Geri Arai and Claudine Fujii at the Hilo Public Library, Reverend Shinryu Akita, Bob Alder, Barbara Andersen, the Arruda family, Lisa Barton at the Laupahoehoe Train Museum, Robert "Steamy" Chow, Patti Cook, Lynn Elia at Lyman Museum, Karyl Franks, Toki Noguchi and Genevieve Cain at the Pacific Tsunami Museum, the Hilo Yacht Club, Bob Hughes, John May, Debbie Fujimoto and KTA Superstores, Macario, Craig Miyamoto, Gail Miyashiro, Ray Mizuba, Alice Moon, Christine and David Reed at Basically Books, Helie Rohner, Charlotte Romo, Jack Roney, Wayne Subica at the Hawaii Plantation Museum, Suisan Fish Company, Steve Todd, Hawea Waia'u, Douglas Yamamoto and everyone else who has helped, in one way or another, to keep the memories of old Hilo alive.

Foreword

When I was a boy, Hilo was a small town where you could get a soda for a nickel and where kids could catch the sampan buses from downtown Mo‘oheau Park to go home from school. I graduated from Hilo High School in 1957, when Elvis was the king and rock-and-roll was our music.

Today, though time and circumstances continue to reshape our community, Hilo is still a small town. These days cruise ships bring large numbers of visitors to our shores to stroll our beautiful, bayfront downtown area and explore our revitalized streets, shops and restaurants. The area's economic base has changed from being largely a sugar plantation model to a 21st-century workforce complete with telecommuters and diversified agriculturalists. And more than ever, new stores and opportunities are becoming available in Hilo, bringing us seemingly closer to our mainland neighbors.

Yet the essence of Hilo remains largely unchanged from times past. Our neighborhoods and business areas are still quiet and friendly. People in Hilo still greet each other on the street with a smile, bring to work avocados and mangos from their overflowing trees, and dress comfortably and casually. Returning from a visit to the bustle of Honolulu reminds us that our traffic is still light, our downtown buildings low, our people relaxed and the pace wonderfully easy. All of this is a part of Hilo's history and is part of what makes it the friendly, easy-going and unique place it is.

And of course the town's history is also preserved in our memories of what has gone before.

That's why this book of old Hilo photos and stories is such a treasure. It preserves the proud heritage of our beautiful town by the bay and keeps those memories alive, even as we create a new history. One that hopefully celebrates the best of what came before us, and builds upon that to help Hilo evolve into an even better town for the generations to come.

Harry Kim
MAYOR, *County of Hawai‘i*

22* Yin Bun Lau Chop Sui

"Hilo sampans" and private vehicles travel Kamehameha Avenue in the 1930s. The sampans—colorful, open-sided jitneys, usually family-owned—provided public transportation on the Big Island for more than a half-century; the last few went out of service in the mid-'70s. Yin Bun Lau Chop Sui was located makai (toward the ocean) of Kamehameha across from Furneaux Lane. This and neighboring structures were not rebuilt after they were destroyed by the tsunami of 1946; today the area is open space. *Hawai'i State Archives*

*** See map, inside back cover.**

Introduction

Hilo's downtown area is lovely and unique, situated as it is at the foot of the venerable volcano Mauna Kea and resting alongside the usually calm and always crescent-shaped Hilo Bay. Gone are the railroad tracks, ramshackle buildings and outermost business-lined streets that, until the mid-1900s, blocked ocean views and breezes. Banned from redevelopment after deadly tsunamis swept across the bay in 1946 and 1960, large swaths of prime bayfront real estate now stand free of homes and commerce. Instead, there are graceful, unencumbered beaches where paddlers hold regattas and house their canoes, and grassy parkland where children play soccer in the sea breeze. Instead of t-shirt and ice cream shops, along its bayfront, sleepy Hilo has a row of tall coconut trees that lead the eye to an early 20th-century gazebo, where the county's band has performed for more than a century and where ethnic cultural clubs still hold well-attended festivals.

Hilo has a rich cultural history that still exists pretty close to the surface. It's in Hilo, at a heiau that stood between the current public library parking lot and the Methodist Church, that Kamehameha is said to have fulfilled a prophecy of uniting the islands by lifting the ancient, weighty Naha stone, which now sits solidly in front of the library. Hilo is also where Kamehameha hunkered down to order his war fleet built—thousands of canoes, by some accounts—with which to conquer the other islands that we now call, collectively, by the Big Island's name: Hawai'i.

In early 19th-century Hilo, whalers and missionaries overlapped and interacted. Whaling captains put in for supplies at the port town and sometimes left their wives in Hilo to wait for them while they went to sea. The Lymans, Christian missionaries who settled in Hilo in the 1830s, entertained whalers, their wives and other Western visitors at their wooden frame house, now part of the Lyman Memorial Museum and one that Westerners, and others, can still visit. The missionaries reshaped Hilo town with a huge wave of their own—just six years after they arrived, neighboring villages were deserted because their inhabitants had relocated to Hilo to take part in the "Great Religious Revival." Hilo's churches, grass structures at first, became progressively larger and more permanent as their congregations' numbers increased dramatically. This religious revival and subsequent migration is what made Hilo the population center it is today.

As whaling declined, sugar geared up. Sugar plantations and mills were built, railroads were constructed to transport cane as well as passengers, and Hilo became the center of the island's commercial sugar industry. Around the turn of the 20th century, immigrants came to the area from China, Japan, Portugal, the Philippines and elsewhere to work on sugar plantations, creating the mélange of linguistic, culinary and cultural traditions that today makes Hilo so rich. By 1900, businesses, shops, restaurants, theaters and other buildings were built and Hilo was a flourishing commercial town. Some of these early 1900s buildings still stand.

The last cane truck rolled off a Big Island sugar plantation in 1995, and then sugar no longer ruled the land. Into the void came diversified agriculture—boutique farms raising heirloom tomatoes, gourmet mushrooms, living lettuce and more than 130 types of tropical fruit, many of them destined for Hilo's widely praised Wednesday and Saturday farmers market. And tourism came too, as each week Hilo welcomes thousands of cruise ship visitors to its shores. Galleries and art studios have also taken root in lush Hilo, which is starting to be known as an art town. Yet, despite its growth, its university and the good restaurants and small but fascinating museums, Hilo remains a small town where residents encounter familiar faces and still sometimes call streets by names that changed decades ago ("Front Street," for instance, for Kamehameha Avenue), and where some parking meters still accept pennies.

What else makes Hilo unique? It's a town where the Hawaiian culture continues to flourish. Not just during the popular week-long Merrie Monarch hula competition each spring, when both ancient and modern hula sway through the town and Hilo fills with dancers, their families and other enthusiasts. Then the town truly looks Hawaiian again, if only for a week, because the Hawaiian faces seem to outnumber other ones. But also during the rest of the year, when hula dancers practice in funky studios next to supermarkets, and a growing number of public school students take classes taught in the poetic Hawaiian language. It's not unusual to hear Hawaiian spoken in Hilo again, sometimes by a parent to a child being reared solely in the language. It's a town whose cultures continue to hold on tight. But at the same time, it's one that is looking forward. A very active community group is working through an impressive list of action items to preserve downtown Hilo's unique history and enhance its future.

This photographic account preserves and celebrates some of that history—the Hilo Boarding School using its irrigation ditch to provide the town with its first electricity; the railroad station that, prior to the 1946 tsunami, sat across from Kamehameha Avenue near the Wailuku bridge; the Saturday morning "Mickey Mouse Club" showings at the Palace Theatre that two and a half decades of Hilo kids remember so well. The old photographs remind us of when the Hilo bayfront was a broad, black sand beach where people rode on horseback, and of the dangers posed by tsunami, which are, statistically speaking, overdue and which next time will strike a generation tragically unaccustomed to their dangers.

These old photos are keyed to the gatefold map at the back of the book. Follow the map's route and you will rediscover historic Hilo, which lies not far below the surface of the present-day town. Encounter a different time and a different landscape, both easily visible if you know where to look. This book will show you where to see vestiges of Hilo's fascinating past.

33* Hilo Railroad Station

Located on Kamehameha Avenue, Hilo's railroad station (left), was also the site of the town's first post office. The depot stood across Kamehameha Avenue from the present Koehnen Building (at photo's right), between Waiānuenue Avenue and Shipman Street. Built to transport sugar from Hāmākua and Puna mills to Hilo Harbor, the railroad also carried passengers. Its Hāmākua route, running between Hilo and Pa'auilo on tracks that crossed 211 waterways, was an engineering marvel. *Ian Birnie Collection*

*** See map, inside back cover.**

Chapter One
The Plantation Era

34 Hilo Railroad Station

Driving from Hāmākua into Hilo town, motorists cross the "singing bridge" over the Wailuku River and then see a "Welcome to Hilo" sign on the right. The sign, which stands next to Kamehameha Avenue and just across from Koehnen's Interiors, is approximately where Hilo's railroad station stood until destroyed in 1946 by a tsunami.

Laupahoehoe Train Museum

41 Railroad Turntable

Previously located at the Hāmākua end of Kamehameha Avenue, near the stone wall that runs along the Wailuku River, the site of the former railroad turntable is now under grass. Hilo historian Robert "Steamy" Chow remembers when, as a teenager in the 1930s, he sold newspapers at nearby Hilo Drug. "I knew the conductor," he says, "and I knew when they were going to turn the thing around. If I wasn't busy, I would run down and help the guy turn it, just to get the short train ride between the station and the turntable." *Kent W. Cochrane/Laupahoehoe Train Museum*

35 Malolo Special

The *S.S. Malolo*, a passenger ship that came to Hilo in the 1920s, operated this special excursion train that chugged right onto the pier to pick up the ship's passengers. Its scenic tour up the Hāmākua Coast to Pa'auilo covered 34 miles. When it exited the half-mile-long tunnel at the Maulua Trestle, suddenly suspended 100 feet in the air over Maulua Gulch, the train stopped to let people take a shocking look down. Here it is heading out of Hilo with the railroad depot at left, and the Wailuku Bridge at the train's fore.

Ian Birnie Collection

SPECIAL
SPECIAL

3 Roundhouse with Locomotives

This quarter-circle structure is the eight-stall, reinforced concrete "roundhouse," or locomotive garage, located at the Hawaii Consolidated Railway's yards in Waiākea. It still stands next to the county swimming pool on Kalanikoa Street, though the tracks and pits where engine parts were hydraulically lowered for repair are gone. Built in 1920, it replaced an earlier, three-stall wooden structure and used the original turntable to reverse the engines into their stalls. The base of the flagpole that previously stood in front of the Hawaii Consolidated Railway office can still be seen makai of Kuawa Street. *Photo by John Mayllan Birnie Collection*

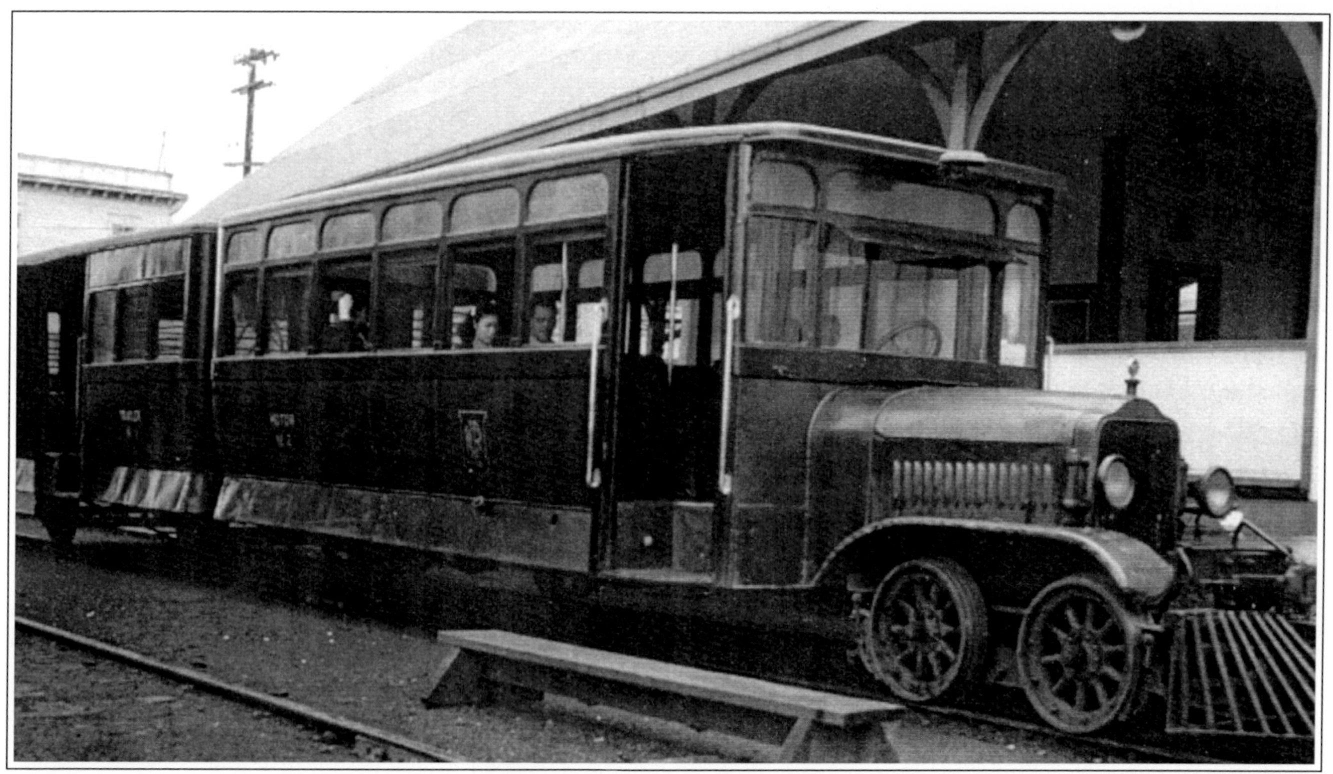

36 Rail Bus and Hilo Station

Passengers rode this "rail bus" between Hilo and Pa'auilo and between Hilo and Pāhoa. Three rebuilt White buses were shipped from the mainland and regular wheels were put on them for transit so they could be easily moved. Upon arrival they were refitted with flanged wheels to enable them to roll over the tracks. *Ian Birnie Collection*

23 Hilo Bayfront Railroad

Tsunamis have hit and damaged downtown Hilo a number of times. This photo shows the railroad, where it ran along the Hilo bayfront, destroyed after a 1923 tsunami. It was repaired, but the tsunami that hit in 1946 marked the end of Hilo's railroad era. *Pacific Tsunami Museum*

11 Hilo Iron Works

Hilo Iron Works, opened in 1865 by William Lydgate and Alexander Young, helped build the landing wharf at the end of Waiānuenue Avenue, many East Hawai'i sugar mills and also the railroad. In 1911, the Iron Works moved into the former Hilo Fruit Company pineapple cannery building next to the Wailoa River. Though the building was damaged (above) in the 1946 tsunami, the long-lived company operated until 1983. Now the renovated, C.W. Dickey-designed building houses various businesses including an art gallery and studios called "Art in the Iron Works." *Pacific Tsunami Museum*

Hāpai Kō

Early "hāpai kō" (Hawaiian for "carry cane") workers were employed by plantations such as the Waiākea Sugar Mill. Laborers came to Hawai'i from China, Norway, Germany, Portugal, Japan, Korea and the Philippines. As quoted in the book ***Pau Hana, Plantation Life and Labor in Hawaii***, one worker recalls becoming a "hapai ko man" in 1920 at age 11: "My first job was loading cane, carrying cane, sugar cane on the back. We built up a bundle about fifty to seventy-five pounds weight and we carry that cane up the ladder into the cane cars." *Laupahoehoe Train Museum*

1 Kuhio Wharf

Ten thousand tons of sugar are stored at Kuhio Wharf on Pier 1 at Hilo Bay, ca. 1923. Railroad tracks ran right into the shed for off-loading the freight, tallied here by the man at left. In the immediate Hilo area, sugar companies included the short-lived, downtown Hawaii Mill Company, which produced sugar in 1901 and 1902 and was located across Kino'ole Street from the present-day fire station, as well as the Hilo Sugar Company, which grew cane in a broad area along the north end of town and beyond. *Hawai'i State Archives/Laupahoehoe Train Museum*

77 **Waiakea Sugar Mill**

The Waiakea Sugar Plantation, pictured here with its rail yard and plantation housing, was unique in that only it and the Wainaku plantation used barges. Waiakea Sugar towed its processed sugar cane through a fishpond and down the Wailoa River to ships at Hilo Bay. Its sugar cane was first planted in 1870 at Waiakea Uka and extended 1,100 feet up Mauna Loa. The 1881-1882 Kīlauea lava flow seriously threatened the plantation; hastily built dikes for diverting lava from the cane fields helped, but still there was considerable damage. The mill ceased operations in 1948, and no remnants remain of the extensive operation, which was located at the corner of Kilauea and Kekuanaoa Streets. *Stanley Heggland, Jr. Collection/Laupahoehoe Train Museum*

39 Wailuku River

The mouth of the Wailuku River opens out, with Hilo Sugar Mill in the Wainaku background. The second-longest river in the Hawaiian Islands, the Wailuku ("Water of Destruction") is said to be the most dangerous. A 19th-century writer noted, "One or more lives have annually been sacrificed to the cataract." Its first bridge, a suspension structure built in 1866, collapsed just seven weeks after its completion when a number of people on horseback, including Richard Dana, author of *Two Years Under the Mast*, were crossing. "Hawaiians fished them out," one person recalled, and no one was injured. *Shipman House Collection*

13 HCR No. 121

Built in 1921 by Baldwin Locomotive Works in Philadelphia, this locomotive, the Hawaii Consolidated Railway No. 121, (known as a "ten wheeler," more specifically a "4-6-0" for its wheel configuration, or a "Casey Jones") carried supplies from the wharves to the sugar mills and then returned with sugar headed for the harbor. *Ian Birnie Collection*

"The knockout blow..."

Nature delivered the knockout blow to the [Hawaii] Consolidated [Railway] at 7 a.m. on April 1, 1946, when the tidal wave struck. A northbound freight pulled by Engine 121 was midway along the bay between the Waiakea yards and the Hilo station when the engineer saw the oncoming fury. He blew his whistle to alert the town and the fireman killed his fire. The first wave pounded into the cab, then receded, and the crew fled across the street and climbed to the roof of a two-story building, escaping with minor bruises. The diabolical power of the second wave derailed three tank cars of gasoline and scattered boxcars inland. Remarkably, the engine stayed on the rails, the track ripped up in front and behind for a mile. When it was all over the Hilo passenger station, freight depot and boxcars spotted nearby were gone, the motor car turntable was torn out, and the first span of the Wailuku River bridge was 600 feet up the river.

– *John B. Hungerford,* Hawaiian Railroads

13 HCR No. 121, 1946

In 1946, a major earthquake off the Aleutian Islands caused a tsunami to race toward Hawai'i at 512 mph. The first wave hit Hilo Bay at 7:01 a.m., just as northbound freight No. 14, hauled by engine No. 121, was on the shoreline tracks about halfway between Waiākea and the Hilo station. When the waves receded, Hilo's bayfront was devastated, with Engine No. 121 the only thing left standing. Its coastal tracks destroyed, Hawaii Consolidated Railway went out of business and a new Hāmākua Coast highway (Hwy. 19) was subsequently built atop the existing railbed.

Lee Hatada Collection/Pacific Tsunami Museum

18 Hilo Town

A 19th-century view of Hilo town from the beach shows Haili Church at right, built in the mid-1850s. J.M. Lydgate described the bayfront area in 1873: "The sea at that time came right up to the bank edge of Front street, so that in heavy weather the spray blew more or less up into the street. Along Front street tall coconut trees of great age towered up over the street. From the foot of Church street extending along the beach it was open country, with the exception of one Hawaiian home, one canoe-builder's workshop—or halau, as it is called by the Hawaiians—and a tumbled down little blacksmith shop some distance farther on." *C.J. Hedemann Collection*

Chapter Two

Markets & Merchants

45 Waiānuenue Avenue

As it does today, Waiānuenue Avenue ca. 1890 ran through some of Hilo's prime commercial area. Note the drainage, with wide ditches draining water to the ocean, and the walkways across them. "Wai Ānuenue" was an old name for what is now called Rainbow Falls, and the dirt horse-and-buggy road was so named because it led to the falls. In 1890 most of the homes above Pitman (now Kinoʻole) Street were still grass houses.

C.J. Hedemann Collection

37 Waiānuenue at Kamehameha

A 1901 article in *Paradise of the Pacific*, the predecessor of *Honolulu* magazine, describes what had developed into one of Hilo's main streets for "leading stores"; "Waianuenue street, beginning at the water front and continuing for several miles to Kaumana, is one of the most attractive in the city. It is on this thoroughfare that the leading stores are situated. It has cement sidewalks for a long distance and the street is sixty feet wide." This photo, looking up Waiānuenue Avenue from Kamehameha Avenue, was taken at the turn of the century. *Koehnen's Collection*

24 Hilo Mercantile Co.

Dating from 1857, the Hilo Mercantile Company operated on Front Street (now Kamehameha Avenue) on a site that was later Hilo Dry Goods and is now the Salvation Army's Sally Shop. Its new building, erected in 1897, featured Hilo's first elevator and sold oils, wallpaper, lumber, lime and cement, sashes, doors, blinds and feed. The company threw a dance for its grand opening. Hilo Mercantile laid railroad tracks from the docks to its lumberyard, and wagon roads allowed customers to drive their wagons in and load up their purchases. Theo H. Davies and Co. bought the company in 1920.

Lyman Museum

43 H. Hackfeld & Co.

This block-long, two-story reinforced concrete building, built by H. Hackfeld in 1910 and now the Koehnen Building, is a local rendition of the Renaissance Revival architectural style. Originally it housed H. Hackfeld & Co., a wholesale general merchandise operation that also encompassed a lumberyard and planing mill, contracting and plumbing departments, furniture making, and marine and fire insurance. During World War I the Germany company's assets were seized and the building was subsequently resold, first to American Factors and then to F.W. Koehnen. Despite having weathered two major tsunamis, its elegant koa staircase inside and native ʻōhiʻa wood flooring still exist within Koehnen's Interiors. *Koehnen's Collection*

52 Von Hamm-Young Building

The event is probably the 1912 grand opening of the Von Hamm-Young Corporation's Buick-Nash-Dodge dealership, which sat on the Hāmākua/mauka corner of what is now Waiānuenue Avenue and Kino'ole Street. The Von Hamm-Young corporation, founded in Honolulu by Conrad von Hammof Berlin and his father-in-law, Alexander Young, brought the first cars, refrigerators, gasoline stations and radios to the Islands. The company also sold dry goods, drugs and insurance, and in 1964 became The Hawaii Corporation. An Internet cafe now stands in a newer building on the site. *Douglas Yamamoto Collection*

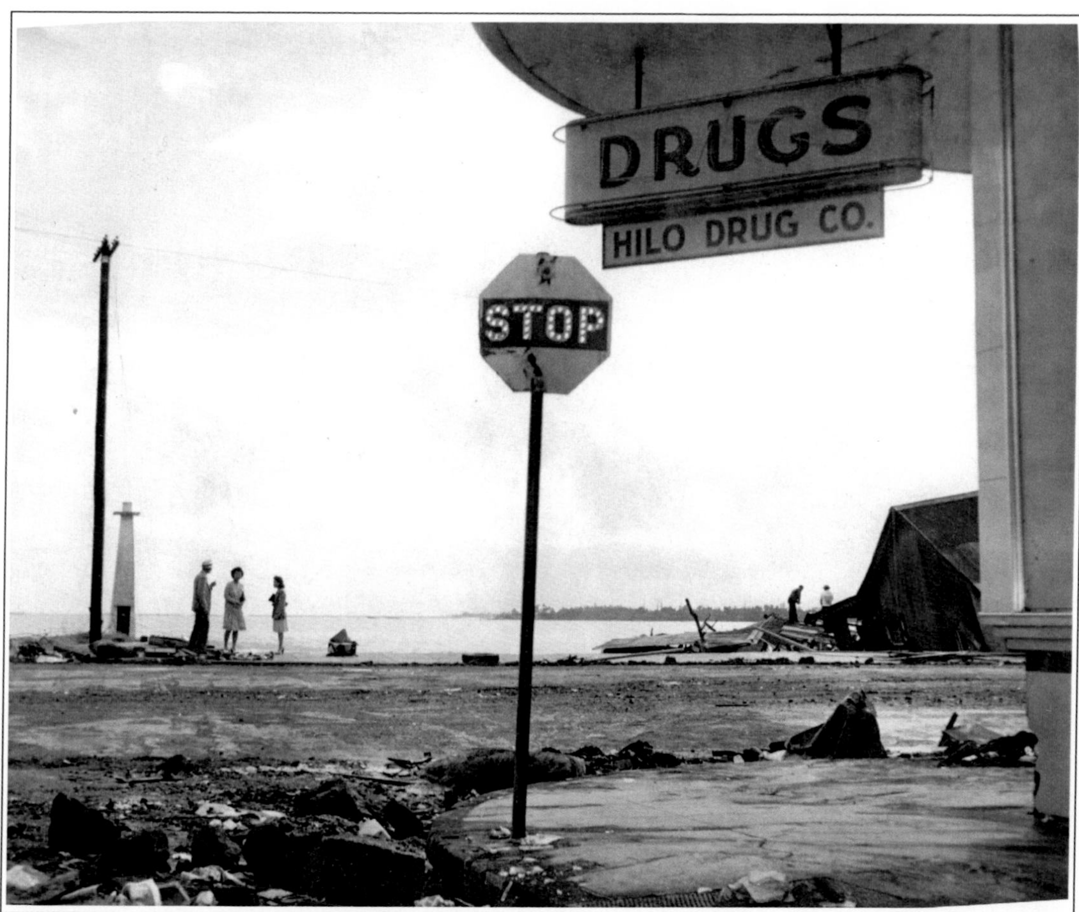

31 Hilo Drug Company
Hilo's first drug store, here ca. 1946, opened in 1896, and a few months later an earthquake almost finished it off. But from that first business arose the Hilo Drug Company founded in 1898, and located at the mauka/Puna corner of Kamehameha and Waiānuenue Avenues. A 1920 newspaper article notes that at that time the store still displayed some of the "old chemical glassware" brought around Cape Horn by Dr. Charles Wetmore, a medical missionary to Hilo who arrived in 1849 and was the first person to dispense Western medicines on the Big Island.
Pacific Tsunami Museum

9 Suisan Fish Market

Started in 1907 by a small group of Waiākea fishermen and seafood brokers, Suisan Fish Market hauled its fish into Hilo by horse-drawn buggy in the early years and sold it in open baskets. After World War II the company expanded into frozen foods, operated a shoyu (soy sauce) and miso brewery and a jam and jelly plant, and began processing guava and other fruit purées. Suisan is now a worldwide import/export operation dealing in fresh and frozen fish, meats, poultry and dairy products.
Suisan Collection

1919
FISH MARKET

30 Kamehameha Avenue, makai

Hilo sampans—the distinctive car/jitney hybrid taxis that served the town from the '30s through the '50s—cruise Kamehameha Avenue before the 1946 tsunami, when stores lined both sides of the street. The makai (toward the ocean) side of the block (right) is gone now, its buildings splintered or shoved across the street into structures on the other side. Just after the tsunami the street was impassable and took on the look of wartime. "Tsunami" is a Japanese word meaning "great wave in harbor." Hawaiians call the destructive waves kai ʻeʻe. The Hawaiian language also has a name (kai mimiki) for the receding of the ocean before the kai ʻeʻe rushes to shore. *Laupahoehoe Train Museum*

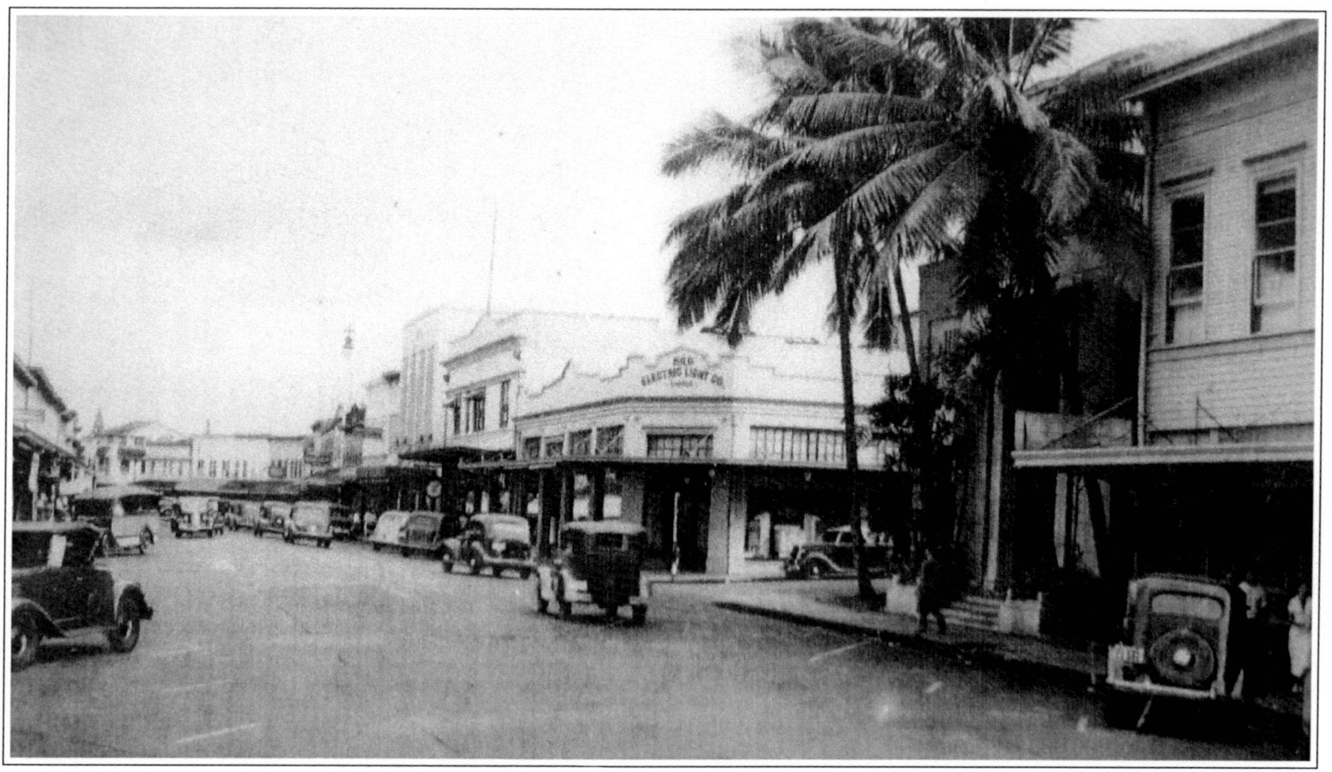

32 Kamehameha Avenue, mauka

This photo shows the mauka (toward the mountains) side of Kamehameha Avenue prior to the 1946 tsunami, looking toward Puna; Kalākaua Avenue is visible toward the photo's right. It's still a familiar view of Kamehameha Avenue except for the structures at left, which were not rebuilt after the tsunami. Ninety-six people in and around Hilo were killed in the 1946 disaster, as well as 24 up the coast at Laupāhoehoe. *Laupahoehoe Train Museum*

12 Shinmachi

Established around 1900, Shinmachi ("New Town" in Japanese) was a close-knit, primarily Japanese community on the mauka side of Kamehameha Avenue. It stretched from the former Piopio Street near the Wailoa River to the Hilo Iron Works. Its low-lying ground had been swampland until it was filled with sand from the Hilo bayfront. In the 1946 tsunami, though, many of the town's buildings were demolished and more than 100 lives were lost. Post-disaster, everything that remained was relocated, and what was formerly Shinmachi is now grassy parkland. *Pacific Tsunami Museum*

75 Hilo Macaroni Factory

Famous for its large, round Saloon Pilot crackers, the Hilo Macaroni Factory operated from 1908 until 2003. It first produced noodles, then added the popular Saloon Pilots when a World War I German ship's baker, during the vessel's detention in the harbor, taught the company's cooks how to bake hardtack. The hard dry crackers, often eaten with butter and sugar, became a Hilo tradition and were sold in packages or tins. The company started on Kamehameha Avenue and moved to its Kino'ole Street location after the 1946 tsunami. *Pacific Tsunami Museum*

21 S. Hata Building

The S. Hata Building (back center, with the 14 arched windows) was built when the area now called Kamehameha Avenue was still swampland, by Mr. and Mrs. Sadanosuke Hata, who came to Hilo from Japan before 1895. Mr. Hata originally operated a horse and carriage business there while his wife had a furoya, or bathhouse, enterprise. By 1912 the Hata Store, which extended to Mamo Street, was selling groceries, hardware and fabric, much of it imported from Japan. During World War II the building (above, after 1946 tsunami) was confiscated as alien property and later put up for auction. The Hatas' daughter repurchased the Renaissance Revival-style building, now part of a family corporation, by sealed bid. *Pacific Tsunami Museum*

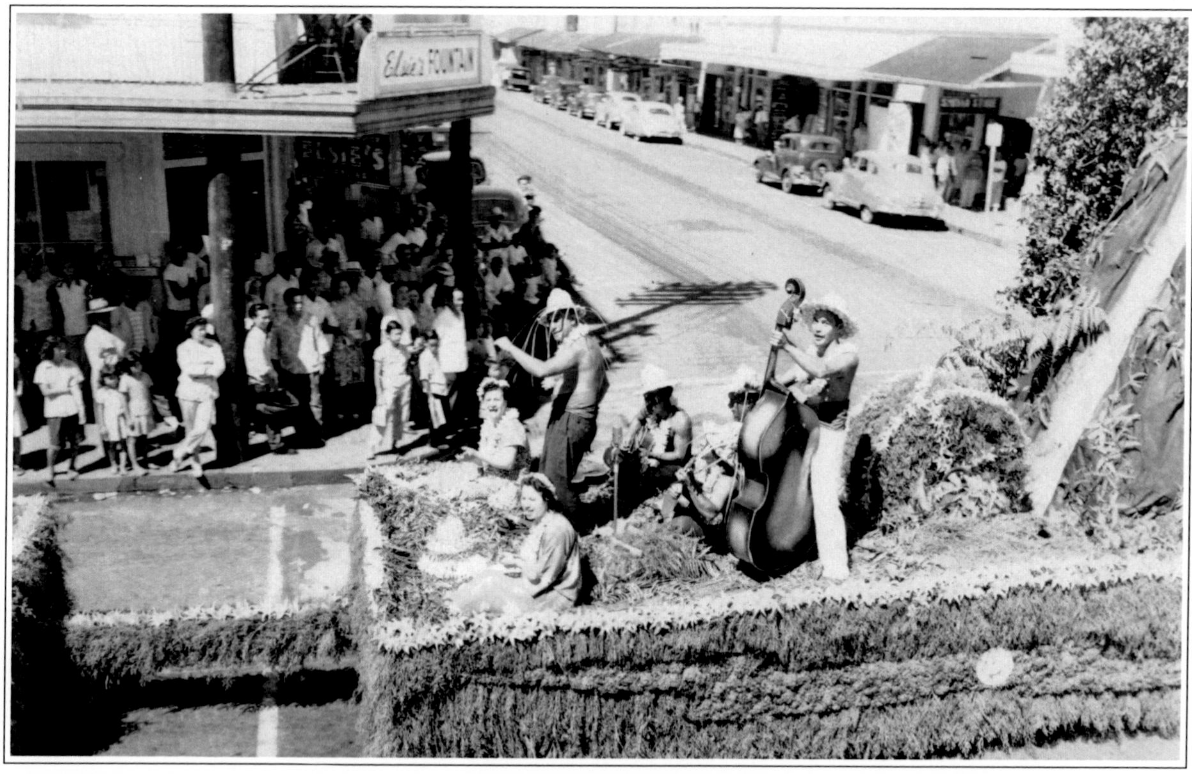

72 Elsie's Fountain

Elsie's Fountain, at the corner of Mamo and Keawe Streets, was opened in the 1940s by Mr. James Shinohara, who always wore a bow tie, a long-sleeved dress shirt and dark trousers. He named the place for his wife, Elsie. Next door to a Japanese public bathhouse and a barbershop at that time, Elsie's (here during a late-1940s Aloha Week Parade) had high stools and a high soda fountain. Closed in 1997, the diner has since changed hands and is now the Ohana Cafe. Along with many other early Hilo artifacts, a stand-on scale from the shop is preserved at Hilo's Plantation Memories Museum. *Pacific Tsunami Museum*

"The smell of the mud..."

We floated in our house like a boat for a good block or two until we got stuck under a mango tree. That's the only thing that kept us from floating on, or out into the ocean. It was terrifying. I was in first grade. It was pitch dark, one in the morning, and we were standing in the living room, knee deep in water, watching everything go by. Well, *we* were going by, really. Our house was right next to the restaurant and we watched the restaurant just explode. The electricity, I guess. At about 5:00, the Red Cross came and pulled us out through windows. To this day I remember the smell of the mud. I can still smell that mud.

– Gail Miyashiro of Cafe 100, on the 1960 tsunami

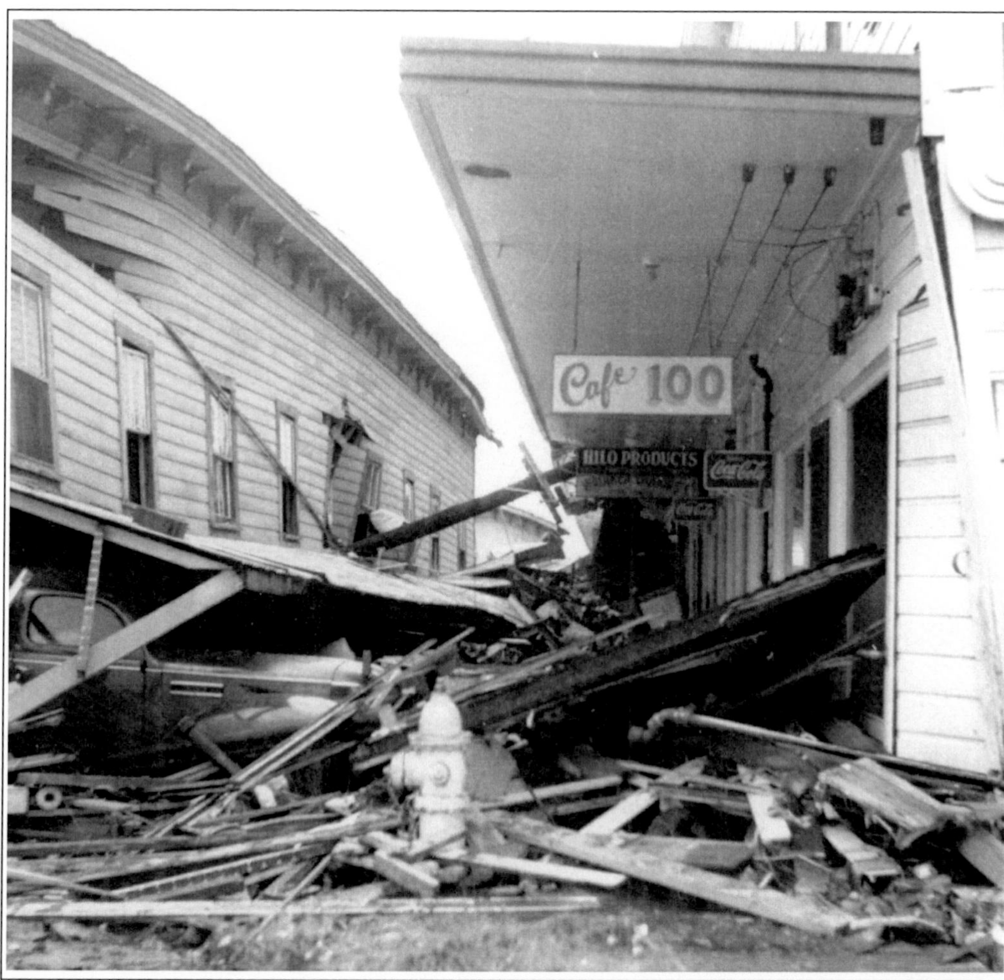

8 Cafe 100

Three months after Richard and Evelyn Miyashiro opened Cafe 100, Hilo's first drive-in, the restaurant at Manono Street and Kamehameha Avenue was damaged by the 1946 tsunami. In May of 1960, three weeks after the family restaurant was relocated to Kamehameha Avenue and Kuawa Street, that restaurant was completely demolished by another tsunami. However, the restaurant seems to have the endurance of the 100th Infantry Army Battalion, Richard's unit during World War II, for which it was named. In 1962, the Miyashiros reopened at their present Kīlauea Street location, where their daughters still operate the landmark restaurant known for its loco mocos and beef stew.

Pacific Tsunami Museum

42 Kamehameha Avenue, mauka

Kamehameha Avenue stretches in the Puna direction, after the 1946 tsunami. After that catastrophe, which killed almost 100 people in and around Hilo and caused $25 million in damage, some homes and business were rebuilt and crowded communities began popping up again without any regard to dangers from future tsunamis—which soon began rolling in again. One hit Hilo in 1952; another in 1957. The bayfront was once again devastated by the 1960 tsunami, which took 61 lives and caused $50 million in damages. *Koehnen's Collection*

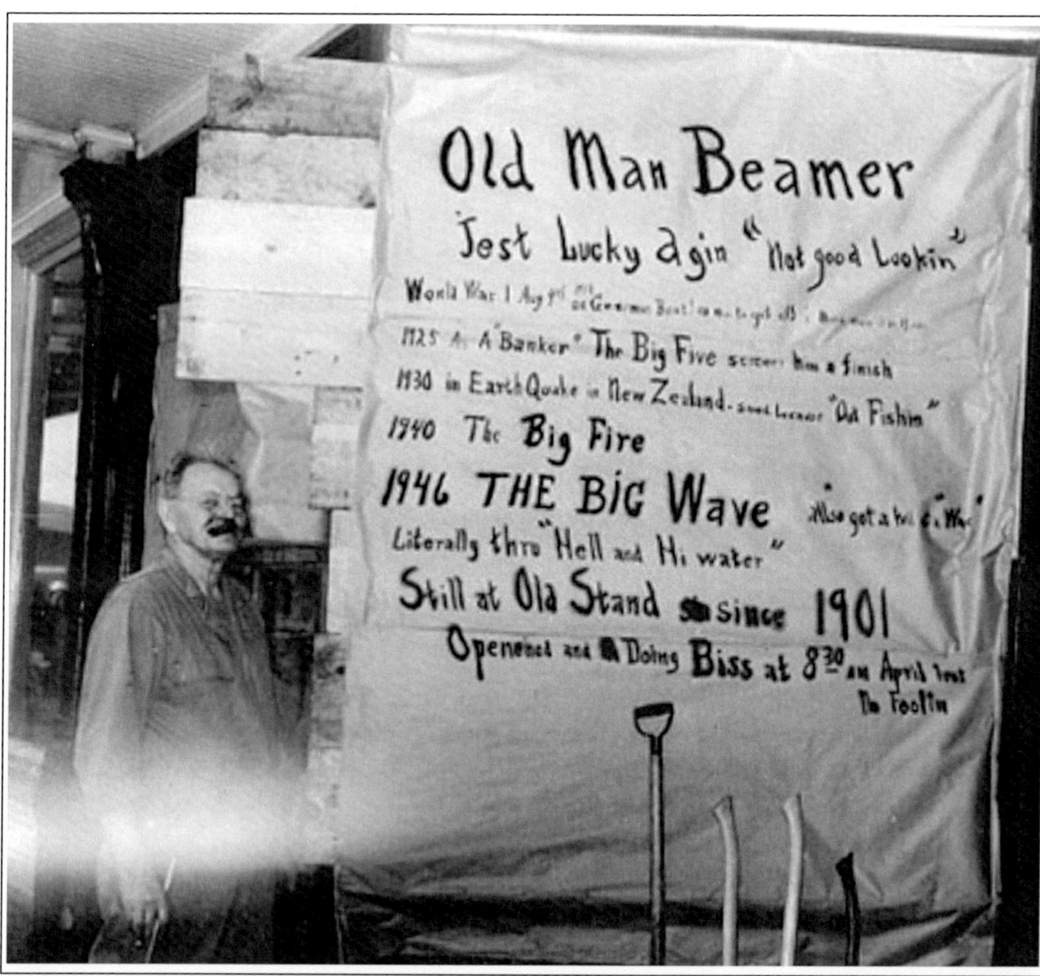

Old Man Beamer
Jest Lucky agin "Not good Lookin"
1940 The Big Fire
1946 THE BIG Wave
Literally thru "Hell and Hi water"
Still at Old Stand since 1901

29 Beamer Store

Pete Beamer, Sr., opened Beamer Store on Front Street (now Kamehameha Avenue) in 1901. In 1899, he was headed to Manila as part of a round-the-world bicycle tour, and made a stopover in Honolulu. He heard about a Kīlauea eruption, visited the Big Island, and never looked back. Beamer stayed on to found the People's Bank, become president of the American Trading Co., and run his store for more than 60 years. The store, with its landmark "old red front," featured much more than its primary stock of tools and hardware. A 1962 *Hilo Tribune-Herald* article mentioned inventory as varied as mid-Victorian hand coffee mills, weavers' wood carders and cowbells. "The house that's got things!" boasted ads.

Pacific Tsunami Museum

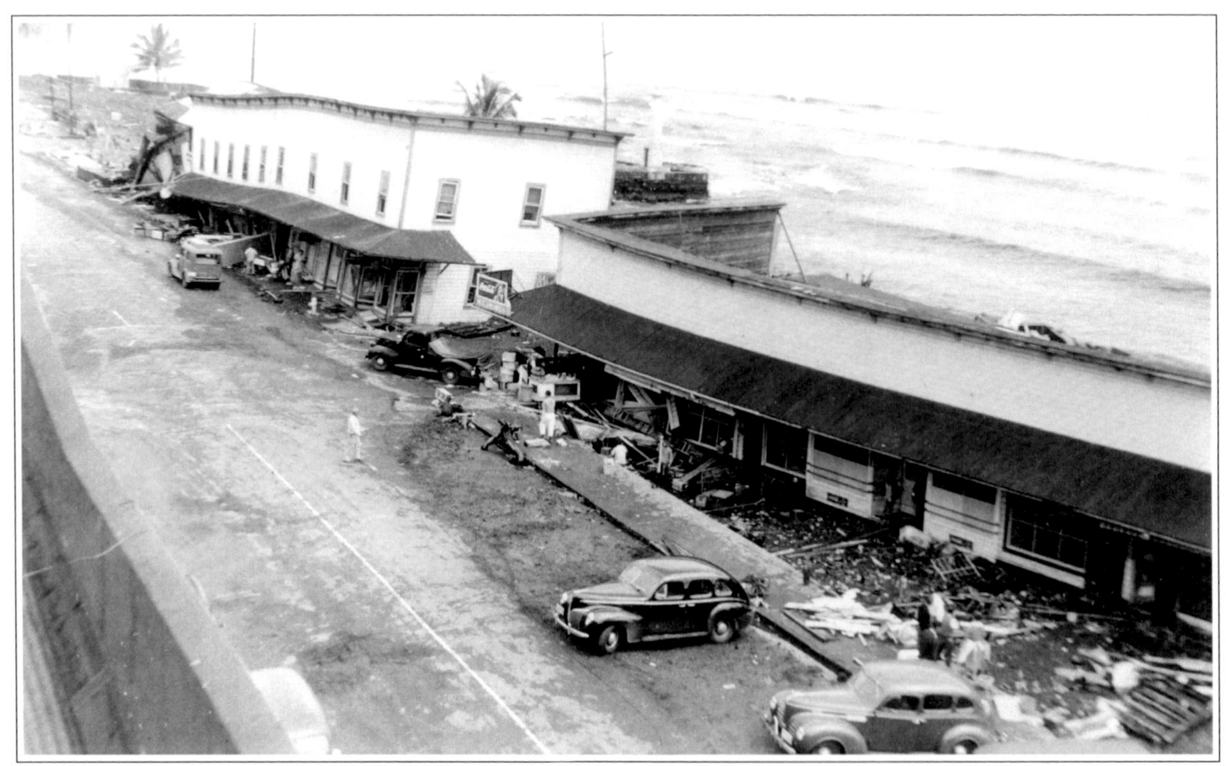

30 Kamehameha Avenue, makai, 1946

The landscape of Hilo changed suddenly and dramatically with the devastating 1946 tsunami. Before it struck, Hilo residents surely couldn't have imagined that an entire long line of buildings—covering several blocks and housing businesses they frequented every day—would soon be simply gone, never to be rebuilt. The buildings lining the mauka side of Kamehameha Avenue formerly lacked the sea views they have now; prior to that disaster, another row of buildings stood along the makai side of the street, as pictured here. *Pacific Tsunami Museum*

71 K. Taniguchi Store, 1939

In 1916, Koichi and Taniyo Taniguchi started the first K. Taniguchi store (now KTA), which sold groceries, fabrics and basic needs, on Lihiwai Street where Suisan Fish Market is now. Later, they added the downtown Keawe Street store (pictured here at its grand opening), and then branches in Kailua-Kona, Puainako, Keauhou and Waimea. During the difficult World War II days of food rationing, the Taniguchis apportioned groceries to make sure people shared equally in what the store was able to get. "Be sure the children have food," they would tell their customers in Japanese. They also extended credit during those hard times, and bills were eventually repaid, some by their customers' children.

Taniguchi Family Collection

27 Kress Building

The Kress building, built in 1932 and pictured after the 1946 tsunami, housed Hilo's popular five-and-dime store until 1980. With its terra cotta facade and terrazzo flooring, the building was Hilo's introduction to the Art Deco style of architecture. U.S. Senator Hiram Fong purchased the structure in 1990 in order to restore the historic building, the only remaining Kress building in the nation, and return it to the community's active business life. Restoration efforts retained the original Art Deco style. Currently the Kress Building houses a charter elementary school, a movie theater and an ice cream shop. *Pacific Tsunami Museum*

25 Hilo Dry Goods

Hilo Dry Goods, located on Kamehameha Avenue where the Salvation Army's Sally Shop is now, was founded in 1915 as a partnership by Lau Fai and his brothers, who came to Hilo from Canton, China. Originally the store sold shoes, dresses and piece goods. Over time, the brothers discontinued this merchandise and began selling gift items. The partnership gradually dissolved, leaving Lau as sole owner. In 1933, his son became manager, and the business (above, after the 1946 tsunami) was incorporated in 1949. *Walter Lesko Collection/Pacific Tsunami Museum*

20 Kwong See Wo

The store Kwong See Wo used to take up most of the block at the mauka/Puna corner of Kamehameha Avenue and Mamo Street. Lee Chau opened the store during the World War I era, and sold an eclectic collection of items including dry goods, food and sundries. As an import house, the store also sold imported goods from China. *Pacific Tsunami Museum*

"Receding sea..."

And now we have another mea hou [news]. A "kai mimiki" [receding sea]. We have had several before, but none just like this. It commenced soon after midnight of Thursday night and the rise and fall of the sea has occurred at regular intervals till the present time for ought I know. What is quite remarkable is, that though the receding of the water was great, the rise was not many feet above high water mark save in the rivers and it was there only that any damage was done. One bridge was carried away and the fish dams much injured. Men who were out fishing say that there were 12 tidal waves, but after day light there was no wave but a quiet receding and returning of the waters. The cause we do not understand....

– *From* The Lymans of Hilo. *An August 15, 1868 letter from Sarah Joiner Lyman, Hilo, to Mrs. Lorenzo Lyons in Waimea, Hawai'i.*

58 Hilo Union School

Hilo Union School was established in 1868 on the Waiānuenue Avenue site where it is still located. It was the first large elementary school in the area, uniting many smaller schools, and in its early years offered two separate departments. In one, instruction was in English and tuition was charged. In the other department, instruction was in Hawaiian and there was no charge. Near the end of the school's chain link fence are two flat lava rocks on the grass, formerly a stone walkway known as the Queen's Walk, where Queen Lili'uokalani used to walk from Niolopa to visit the Rufus Lyman family. *Hilo Union School Collection*

Chapter Three

School Days

59 Hilo Intermediate School

When Hilo High School moved to its current location in 1923, what was then called Hilo Junior High School (now Hilo Intermediate) took over the former high school campus, located across Waiānuenue Avenue from Hilo Union School. When the junior high school outgrew that site, its current school buildings were built, opening in 1929. A stream that Hawaiians previously used for taro irrigation still runs under the current school's site, along the makai end of the Hilo High School track field, and then empties into the Wailuku River. *Hawai'i State Archives*

78 Kapi'olani School Originally called Piopio School, Chiefess Kapi'olani Elementary School on Volcano Road (now Kīlauea Avenue) was built in 1920. Its name changed in 1923. When built, it was a six-room schoolhouse with a lavatory. More property was acquired and additions built, and in 1928, it was the only school on the island with a projection room for showing moving pictures. By 1930, the school grounds included 22 acres. After the Pearl Harbor attack, the school closed temporarily and the U.S. Army built barracks at the back of the campus.
Mattie Wakefield Collection, Lyman Museum

"Students from the country dropped out..."

Hilo High, which recently celebrated its 100-year anniversary, has seen a lot of changes over the years. Here are some memories from the book *Hilo High School—"First" 100 Years* by Wayne A. Subica:

"Twenty female students started the Hilo High Lunch Club in 1913, to provide lunch for students who either went home or went into town for lunch. The girls were furnished with an oil stove, a refrigerator, pots and pans, dishes, two tables and few other things. They made potato salad, fruit salad, beef stew, chicken curry, bread pudding, etc. The lunches were good and attracted teachers and students from the Hilo Union School which was located across the street....The first month the club made a profit of $40, with $35 divided among the girls just before Christmas and $5 used to pay for the picture of the Lunch Club members used in the annual, taken at Kilauea Art Studio."

"In 1916, Hilo High started a poultry operation with four incubators, with a hatching capacity of one thousand eggs. Within a few months they added three new incubators which increased the hatching capacity to 1625 eggs. The students also set over 7000 eggs and over 5000 chicks hatched... The demand for the one day old chicks was so heavy that they had no chicks to put into the new brooder house until the following year."

"In 1942, many of the seniors at Hilo High did not graduate because many of the students from the country dropped out of school. They were not allowed to travel on the highway [due to martial law]. After fifty years the Hilo High senior class of 1942 was honored and received their diplomas along with the Hilo High class of 1992."

60 Hilo High School

Hilo High School, here ca. 1908, was the first high school on the Big Island. Before it opened, students wanting an education beyond the eighth grade had to travel to, and board on, Oʻahu. Josephine Deyo, then principal of Hilo Union School, wanted to find a way to keep those students home and allow them to continue their education, and so Hilo High School started with 25 ninth-graders on the grounds of Hilo Union in 1905. In 1906, it moved to a Waiānuenue Avenue location, now a grassy area makai of where the District Annex is situated. In 1923, the school moved to its present Waiānuenue Avenue location. *Wayne Subica Collection*

74 St. Joseph School

St. Joseph School was founded in 1869; in 1900 the Franciscan Sisters from New York arrived to run the school as an all-girls' school with grades one through three, while the Marianist Brothers ran St. Mary's School for boys. In 1948, the two Catholic schools were merged into one for grades three through ten, and the following year the new school was finished on Ululani Street. The only Catholic school on the island, it now accepts both male and female students, from toddler age through 12th grade. *Arruda Family Collection*

63 Hilo Boarding School, ca. 1904

Congregational missionaries David and Sarah Lyman arrived in Hilo in 1832, and four years later they opened the Hilo Boarding School (located on Haili Street where the Boys and Girls Club now stands), with seven pupils. Its goal was to educate Hawaiian boys "in the ways of industry and morality" and to be a preparatory school for Lahainaluna High School on Maui. Later, boys of all nationalities were admitted. Over the years students cultivated food crops and sugar cane and ran a tailoring shop, a dairy, a print shop, a blacksmith shop and more. Thought to have been the first industrial training school in the United States, it operated until 1925. *Lyman Museum*

69 Haili Street and Central Christian Church, ca. 1900

Haili Street, named for the forest in Panaewa where the timber used to construct Haili Church came from, was originally called Church Street for its preponderance of churches. This photo, taken in the early 1900s, shows the Portuguese Protestant Church, established in 1892. In early Hilo there were "sister" Christian churches, each ministering to a different population, such as the Japanese Christian Church, the Chinese Christian Church, and others. In 1935, this church changed its name to the Central Christian Church and still stands at the corner of Haili Street and Kīlauea Avenue. *Laupahoehoe Train Museum*

CHAPTER FOUR
Churches of Hilo

66 St. Joseph Church

An early St. Joseph Church, built by Jesuit fathers in 1857 with hardwood plugs instead of nails, was located at Keawe Street and Kalākaua Avenue where the Pacific Building now stands. The earliest church structures built for the first Catholic missions in Hilo were grass chapels. The current St. Joseph Catholic Church, built on Haili Street in 1917, was designed by Honolulu architect E.A.P. Newcomb in the style of old mission architecture. Its clock, made by the Seth Thomas Clock Company in Thomaston, Connecticut, chimed on the half hour around the clock until nearby residents complained.

C.J. Hedemann Collection

68 First Foreign Church

The first building in the line of churches leading to today's First United Protestant Church was the "Seaman's Bethel," a stone building constructed to minister to sailors from whaling ships that anchored in Hilo Bay. In 1868, Kamehameha V granted a charter for what was then called the First Foreign Church, and this church building was built at the corner of Kino'ole and Haili Streets. It was rebuilt in 1897, and in 1954 the church's name was changed to First United Protestant Church. Stones from the original Seaman's Bethel have been incorporated into each successive church building. *C.J. Hedemann Collection*

"Eighty men to transport a tree..."

The people of the Hilo district began to lay plans for building a new (third) meeting house of 'more ample dimensions.' The second church, although only three years old, was beginning to show signs of age and need of repair. It was also too small for the growing congregation. So the cutting of timber for the new building began. 'The amount of labor must evidently be great,' Goodrich wrote, 'when it is considered that the sticks used for posts are numerous; that the largest are 70 feet long; that they are dragged five miles from high ground of manual labor; and that 80 men are sometimes put in requisition to transport a single tree. Yet, in these labors do the people engage with great alacrity, that they may have a convenient place in which they may worship God.

– *From* Haili Church, 150 Years, *published in 1974*

67 Haili Church

Haili Church's roots go back to a site near the present Hilo Iron Works where stood a thatched grass building (which seated more than 1000 "in a close packed manner") operating as the first church of Hilo's Christian mission station. It was constructed of ʻohiʻa timbers, transported from an upper Waiākea forest called Haili Kulamanu by native church members who hewed, stripped and hauled the wood while chanting traditional chants. At one point, services were held in a thatched building at Kalākaua Park. In the mid-1850s, the king's workmen, who worked two-and-a-half days per week on public projects, started construction on the current Greek Revival-style church at Haili Street.

Hawaiʻi State Archives

70 Taishoji Soto

This first photo of Hilo's Taishoji Soto Mission was taken in 1918 during the visit of Reverend Kenshu Murakami. First established with 800 members in a rented Shinmachi house in 1916, the mission built this structure two years later. At the onset of World War II, the temple's reverend and his family, along with several other board members, were sent to detention camps at Kilauea Military Camp and later on the mainland. Iwajiro Miyashita was approved by the Provost Marshall to stay at the temple (above and opposite) and watch over it during the war years, when its congregation was prohibited from gathering. Today its membership includes 300 families. *Taishoji Soto Mission Collection*

49 Hilo Hotel

This first incarnation of the Hilo Hotel sat on what is now Kinoʻole Street. In 1884, a ten-room hotel with two baths and several small cottages was built (above, ca. 1900). Twenty years later George Lycurgus, who came to Hawaiʻi from Greece in 1889, purchased the property and established a new Hilo Hotel, which boasted "a shower and bath for every room!" Many well-known personalities from the Islands and elsewhere stayed there. Niolopa ("Royal Enclosure"), which was sometimes called "Kalakaua's Summer Palace" and was a retreat for royals (particularly Keʻelikōlani and Kalākaua) in the mid-19th century, was previously located at the rear of the site. *Laupahoehoe Train Museum*

Chapter Five

Small Town Services

"Ice full of bubbles..."

My recollection as to the first use of electric lights in the town of Hilo dates back to about the year 1890. At about that time W.S. Terry, the joint principal with Mrs. Terry of the Hilo Boarding school, put in a small dynamo to light the school buildings.... This was a small direct current machine, driven by water power, and capable of handling not much over a dozen lights, or of just the capacity to light the study hall and the principal's cottage. This machine operated until about 10 p.m. each night then closed down.... In connection with the light plant, a half-ton ice plant had also been installed at the boarding school. With the small plant the needs of the town for ice were supplied. This ice was rather porous and full of air bubbles, who cared; it was ice and people wanted it and proceeded to order it. Delivery was made in a small push cart propelled by the school boys before and after school hours.

– *Levi Lyman,* Hilo Tribune-Herald, *1931*

55 Hawaiian Electric Ice Plant

A 1,000-pound ice block was made by Hilo Electric Light Company, formed in 1895 by Hilo Boarding School trustees who connected a water-driven Dynamo to the school's irrigation ditch. The company provided the area's first electricity (when it offered to furnish and install electric lamps and wires, free, to anyone who agreed to try electricity for six months). Hilo Electric was also the first to offer ice on the Big Island with the opening of the half-ton ice plant. *Lyman Museum*

4 Ho‘olulu Park

The grand opening of Ho‘olulu Park was held on July 4, 1900. The grandstand held 1,000 people, and another 2,000 spectators could sit in open bleachers. The Waiākea park had tracks for horse racing and fields for athletic events. The first motorcycle race in Hilo, won by Pete Beamer, and the park's only automobile races, featuring both male and female drivers, were held in 1911. The grandstand was demolished and the park abandoned in 1913. A new grandstand was built in the '20s; the grounds were cleared and the racetrack restored. It is still used for ballgames.

Hawai‘i State Archives/ Wayne Subica Collection

PARK

19 Mo'oheau Hall

Mo'oheau Park, on the bayfront, is thought to have been named for the chief Ka'ai'awa'awa-i-Mo'oheau, the son of Ho'olulu, who is said to have hidden Kamehameha's bones. The land was donated to the territory by the chief's descendant "Admiral" George Beckley. Its pavilion was dedicated in 1904 to the first public rendition of "The Mo'oheau March," written for the occasion by the Hawai'i County Band's first director. Over the years, the pavilion has been used as a schoolroom and has hosted many rallies and fundraisers. The Hawai'i County Band still performs there. *Laupahoehoe Train Museum*

42 Hilo Armory

Hilo's first National Guard unit formed in 1900, and in 1905 it built and dedicated an armory building on Shipman Street. In 1930, the original one-story wooden structure was demolished and today's Hilo Armory was built on the same site. Until the Hilo Field House (today the Afook Chinen Civic Auditorium) was built in the 1950s, the Armory was only large public building and gym in town, and all high school league games were played there. The building is still in use. *Lyman Museum*

46 Burns Building

Originally built in 1913 to house three lower-level stores and an upstairs rooming house, the carefully restored Burns Buildi at the corner of Waiānuenue Avenue and Keawe Street, still offers rooms for rent upstairs, now as the Hilo Bay Hostel. Back 1913, the two-story wooden structure was a grand facility, with its wide wooden staircase leading to a second floor with wo wainscoting and 13-foot ceilings. Rooms at "The Burns," considered a high-class lodging house, opened off the airy commc area, as they still do today. In 1942, the building became headquarters for the island's United Service Organizations (USO)

Bishop Museum

47 Courthouse

Located at the site of today's fishpond at Kalākaua Park, this building was an all-in-one U.S. Post Office, courthouse and Territorial tax office. The rear of St. Joseph Church can be seen behind the courthouse building.

C.J. Hedemann Collection

53 Hilo Library/Kulana Na'auao

Hilo's first library was organized in 1880 by a private group called the Hawaii Reading Association, and its name was later changed to the Hilo Library and Reading Room Association. In 1899, the library was located in a small church building. Its first librarian was Luther Severance, the son of missionary parents who was also the town's postmaster and sheriff. The first library, with 400 books in its collection, was supported by donations and subscriptions. In 1912, the library moved to Kulana Na'auao, pictured here, and became part of the government's library system. Today this building houses government offices, and the library is located on Waiānuenue Avenue. *Theodore Kelsey/Lyman Museum*

Electric Car - Hilo Post Office circa 1930

50 Hilo Post Office

This small Eklund Exide electric car, built by Walter Eklund in 1924, was featured in fairs throughout the territory. Here it's driven in front of the post office, ca. 1930, located at the federal building. The first letter ever sent from Hilo by air mail was mailed at the Hilo Post Office on October 4, 1934. "The Inter-Island Airways plane will leave Honolulu at 8 a.m. next Monday," advised a newspaper article, "and arrive in Hilo at the Waiakea airport at 11 a.m. The plane will return to Honolulu at 2:30 p.m." Letters could be sent by air mail, in specially marked envelopes, for six cents. *Pacific Tsunami Museum/Wayne Subica Collection*

26 Palace Theatre

From the early 1930s through the mid-1950s, scores of Hilo kids, like those in this 1933 photo, attended the Palace Theatre's "Mickey Mouse Club" hosted by musician Johnny De Mello. Craig Miyamoto remembers: "Every Saturday morning, hundreds of kids would converge on the Palace Theatre.... And for just ten cents, we would spend the next three hours in a world of fantasy. Most of the kids would bring 15 cents, enough for the movie and a small package of crack seed." *John de Mello Collection, courtesy of Roger Angell and Lyman Museum/Bob Alder Collection*

"Wicker armchairs and linen cushions..."

The Palace Theatre on Haili Street was built in 1925 by Adam C. Baker, a well-known showman in Hawai'i and nephew of the last royal governor of the island.

The Big Island's first big theatre, it was built during the heyday of American movie palaces and was said to be the grandest one outside of Honolulu. Its structure was built entirely of redwood imported from the Pacific Northwest. Outside, the facade is an elegant, neo-classical design. Inside, its style is Art Deco. The best seats in the house had wicker armchairs and linen cushions.

Until a sound system arrived in 1928, the theatre showed silent movies and an organist played live pipe-organ music. To this day, before a show starts the audience is treated to live music from a restored pipe-organ.

Consolidated Amusement Company bought the theatre and operated it from 1930 to 1982, after which it sat empty until 1990. Now under restoration, the Palace screens art house movies and hosts live performances.

51 Federal Building

The Federal Building, located across Waiānuenue Avenue from Kalākaua Park, was designed by architect Henry Whitfield in the Classical Revival style. Its original structure was built in 1915, and its two U-shaped wings were added in 1936. Today included on the National Register of Historic Buildings and Places, it now houses government offices, including the downtown branch of the post office. The building's site was formerly the home of Luther Severance, the first postmaster, who held that job for 33 years and was also sheriff. *Hawai'i State Archives*

48 Police Station and Hilo Courthouse

Formerly the courthouse and police station, this building, dedicated in 1932, now houses the East Hawai'i Cultural Center. County engineer Frank Arakawa, a Stanford University graduate who was in the first graduating class of Hilo High School, designed it in the style of a Hawaiian grass house of the mid-1800s, when foreign influences brought higher doors, certain types of windows, wood floors, partitions and verandas. Hilo's courtroom relocated when the State building was completed in 1969. The police department moved from the building in 1975. *Pacific Tsunami Museum*

16 Hilo Bay

In 1903 the editors of *Paradise of the Pacific*, predecessor to today's *Honolulu* magazine, wrote: "Hilo's commercial advancement in the past two or three years has been marked by extensive wharf improvements and the shipment by steam of most of the products of the island of Hawaii, such as sugar, coffee and fruit, directly to San Francisco. By the same new facilities of exporting the means of procuring merchandise from the coast are rendered easier and cheaper. Since 1899 the cost of living in Hilo has been reduced 25 percent, on account of closer relations with the mainland."

C.J. Hedemann Collection

CHAPTER SIX

On the Waterfront

38 Wailuku River

Pre-bridge, the raging Wailuku River was sometimes a formidable barrier between Hilo town and its more agrarian Hāmākua coast neighbors. In 1822, the English missionary William Ellis described people bringing goods—hogs, tobacco, kapa, lauhala mats, kalo—to the banks of the river, then shouting their barters across. Articles of trade were taken to a rock in the middle of the river for the exchange. Ellis wrote: "The banks of the Wairuku [Wailuku] must often have presented an interesting scene, in the bustle of which these clerks of the market must have had no inconsiderable share." *C.J. Hedemann Collection*

"The slipping of travelers..."

The first bugbear in going northward [from Hilo] on the Laupahoehoe trail was the Wailuku river. The trail led down into the bed of the river along the line of Jail [later Kino'ole] street, and back of Mr. F.S. Lyman's present premises. Here the stream rushes, when in ordinary water, through two narrow channels and then leaps over a fall of ten to fifteen feet. Across these were laid foot wide planks on which pedestrians could cross on foot. Horses had to swum across some distance above and their trappings were carried across the planks, or as was sometimes the case, taken down to near the mouth of the river and there swum across to the Puueo shore. The crossing on foot wide planks, with the rushing waters beneath tearing through these narrow channels, was very precarious, and especially so when the planks were muddy and slippery. Some lives had been lost by the slipping of travelers from the planks. Once in the stream, which ran with the velocity of a millrace, life was gone. No one was ever known to be saved after falling into it.

– From "Forty Years' Reminiscence of Life in Hilo, Hawaii" by D.H. Hitchcock, published in the Hilo Hawaii Herald, *May 27, 1897*

37 Hilo Landing

Landing wharves, to help in the ocean transport of goods and passengers, were built between 1863 and 1890 at the foot of what is now Waiānuenue Avenue. D.H. Hitchcock and Sheriff Coney built the first small boat wharf for about $300, then charged vessels $3 per trip to use. A couple of years later, the government reimbursed part of the cost and built a bigger landing. Hitchcock later wrote: "Our little wharf was a vast improvement on the old style of running the boats up onto the sand beach and transferring passengers and goods from them to dry land on the backs of the stalwart boat boys, stripped to their 'malos.'" *C.J. Hedemann Collection*

15 Hukilau

Men gather fish from Hilo Bay in the traditional style of net fishing called hukilau. Akule, papio, moi, mullet, awa and ʻōʻio were caught this way. A kapu (restriction) on aku fishing for half the year, and on ʻōpelu the other half—both fish which seasonally frequent the waters outside Hilo Bay—was regularly observed until the kapu system was overthrown after the 1819 death of Kamehameha I. *C.J. Hedemann Collection*

"A very pleasant vehicle..."

July 30. Took a walk with Mr. Coan to the Royal fish ponds, at the S.E. part of the harbor. They are of brackish water, rise and fall with the tide, and altogether cover several hundred acres. They are generally shallow, but in places of considerable depth. The fine mullet with which they are filled are tabu to all but Royal hooks or nets, and tho' they are innumerable and large, neither natives nor foreigners can often get a taste of them. I saw them collected in a corner of one of the ponds as thick as they could be crowded together, and watched their motions for some time. They are a fine looking fish about a foot long, black on the back, with belly white—occasionally they swim on the back with belly up, and seem to enjoy the change, if one may judge from their lazy, satisfied kind of motion in that position.

The ponds are navigated by rush canoes—made simply of large bundles of tall bulrushes which grow on the banks. They are fan shape, about 6 feet long and 2 or 3 feet wide at the stern. They afford a very pleasant vehicle for the single person. We crossed the pond on a couple of them, enjoyed a bath tho' the water was cold, and returned before tea.

– Chester Smith Lyman, 1846

76 Waiākea Pond

The spring-fed fishponds in Waiākea River were once referred to as the Royal Ponds and were stocked primarily with ʻamaʻama (mullet) and awa (milkfish), caught at the mouths of streams along Hilo Bay. Certain ponds held fish reserved for certain monarchs—for instance, the mullet in one pond belonged to Kaʻahumanu and her descendants. The fishponds were cared for with traditional ritual, and occasionally excess algae was removed from large ponds such as Waiākea by communal labor. In 1823 stone walls encircled the Waiākea ponds and small huts sheltered pond caretakers. *C.J. Hedemann Collection*

14 Black Sand Beach

A wide black sand beach once fronted Hilo Bay, here shown with the two-story Holmes Store (center) and the landing wharf. Opposite, a man chops firewood ca. 1890. In the late 1800s, this was the scene at the foot of Waiānuenue Avenue between the area of the Kress Building and Hilo Drug. Today the black-sand beach, which previously stretched all around the bay to the Wailoa Estuary, lies buried beneath Kamehameha Avenue, parking lots and the Bayfront Highway.
C.J. Hedemann Collection

40 Damaged Wailuku Bridge

On March 31, 1923, "on a perfectly calm day and without warning," according to a Hawaii Consolidated Railway report, ten concrete piers holding up the Wailuku River bridge disappeared into the water. "The cause of this accident is hard to explain, as this bridge had been in service 13 years," the report noted. Five months later, after repairs, a huge storm damaged those piers and several others, and careful examination determined that the bridge needed to be replaced. The railroad put up a temporary span until a steel railroad bridge was completed in 1924. *Laupahoehoe Train Museum*

54 Wailuku Railroad Bridge

This view is of the Wailuku River looking toward the sea, from the Wainaku bridge toward the Pu'u'eo Street bridge and the Wailuku railroad bridge, on April 1, 1946. The river bed is refilling from the next tsunami wave coming upriver. The missing third span of the Wailuku railroad bridge can be seen in the river in front of the Pu'u'eo bridge; it came to rest on the rock formation known in Hawaiian legend as Maui's Canoe, where it sat for several years until it was recovered as scrap metal. *Lawrence Nakagawa Collection/Pacific Tsunami Museum*

2 Molasses Tanks

Another casualty of the 1946 tsunami was a boat, CG-3927, that crashed into the molasses tanks at Hilo Harbor. The sugar plantations produced molasses, and the sugar growers association split the costs of maintaining molasses tanks at the harbor, and operating tank pumps and lines, based on the percentage of sugar they shipped. Molasses was shipped out of Hilo Harbor until 1996, on Matson ships carrying sugar and also on Matson cargo barges, which sometimes used the molasses as ballast. That year, sugar grower C. Brewer & Co. demolished the tanks and removed the lines. *Walter Lesko Collection/Pacific Tsunami Museum*

"Ever since I have been a missionary..."

I have said nothing about molasses. They work some of it over and reduce it to sugar, and each planter ships a few thousand dollars' worth of it, and...feeds the third quality to his hogs, if he has any. Formerly inferior molasses was always thrown away, but here, lately, an enlightened spirit of progress has moved the Government to allow the erection of three distilleries, I am told, and hereafter it will be made into whiskey. (That remark will be shuddered at in some quarters. But I don't care. Ever since I have been a missionary to these islands I have been snubbed and kept down by the other missionaries, and so I will just bring our calling into disrepute occasionally by that sort of dreadful remark. It makes me feel better.)

– Mark Twain, after touring Maui sugar plantations in 1866,
Mark Twain's Letters from Hawai'i.

6 Coconut Island

Coconut Island is a nickname for the small islet in Hilo Bay that Hawaiians call Moku Ola ("Island of Health"). According to the Keli'ipios, the family that served as the island's caretaker from 1905 until their home there was destroyed by the tsunami in 1960, it was named for an underwater rock believed to have healing powers. In ancient times, Moku Ola, along with some of the adjacent shoreline, encompassed a large heiau including a heiau luakini (temple for human sacrifice), a pu'uhonua (place of refuge) and a place of healing.

C.J. Hedemann Collection

10 Wailoa River

An executive governor's order transferred Wailoa River Park from the Territory to the County of Hawaii in 1920, and 88 acres—including Waiākea Fishponds on its makai side—were set aside to become public park. Not until the 1946 tsunami, though, was the land actually cleared of dwellings and squatters. Planning and construction began for a Hawaiian village, which was destroyed by the 1960 tsunami. Later in the '60s, restrooms, parking, barbecue facilities and drinking fountains were added. Soccer fields were dedicated in 1995.

C.J. Hedemann Collection

7 Breakwater

Before Hilo's breakwater was constructed and ships could safely anchor in the bay, 100-pound bags of sugar were ferried out to ships by lifeboat. The Hilo railroad and 'Ōla'a sugar companies lobbied Congress for a breakwater, promising in exchange to extend the railway up the Hāmākua Coast. Started in 1908, the project incorporated about 950,000 tons of rock, quarried from around the island. Built in sections, it was completed in 1929 at a cost of $2.8 million. The 1946 tsunami destroyed 60 percent of the mile-long breakwater, tossing boulders, some weighing more than eight tons, onto the shore. *Hawai'i State Archives*

"A screaming roar..."

Then the tsunami of 1960 came in with a screaming roar which those who heard will never forget. This finished the job begun in 1946.... The voice of reason and experience prevailed. The town must be moved back. The wave swept area must be left for flood zone and recreation, except for the new highway, which took the place of the defunct railroad. Project Kaiko'o (Big or Stormy Sea) came into being. Originally it was supposed to take in land clear to the Wailuku but there were not enough funds available so the Mamo Street line was arbitrarily drawn. This does not mean that the buildings fronting the bay are safe there. They are not, though most were not so severely damaged as those in the Kaiko'o area.

– *Helen Shiras Baldwin,* Hilo Tribune-Herald, *June 23, 1974*

64 Grass House

In 1823, the English missionary William Ellis estimated that 2,000 people lived near Hilo Bay in 400 houses (perhaps such as this one, pictured). Most of these houses were thatched with lauhala, and Ellis wrote that it was surprising, "the despatch with which a house is sometimes built. We have known the natives to come with their materials in the morning, put up the frame of a middling-sized house in one day, cover it in the next, and on the third day return to their lands.... It is no unusual thing to see upwards of a hundred men at a time working on one house." *C.J. Hedemann Collection*

Chapter Seven

Home Sweet Hilo

"An interminable croquet game..."

There is a large native population in the village, along the beach, and on the heights above the Wailuku River. Frame houses with lattices, and grass houses with deep verandahs, peep out everywhere from among the mangoes and bananas. The governess of Hawaii, the Princess Ke'elikolani, has a house on the beach shaded by a large umbrella-tree and a magnificent clump of bamboos, 70 feet in height….

There are two stores on the beach, and at these and at the Court-house [the gentlemen] congregate, for lack of club-house and exchange. Business is not here a synonym for hurry, and official duties are light; so light, that in these morning hours I see the governor, sheriff, and judge, with three other gentlemen, playing an interminable croquet game on the Court-house lawn. They purvey gossip for the ladies, and how much they invent, and how much they only circulate, can never be known!

– *Isabella Bird,* Six Months in the Sandwich Islands, *1875*

73 Nawahī Homes

These homes, surrounded in taro and thought to be on Kapi'olani Avenue, were owned and rented out by the native Hawaiian lawyer and legislator Joseph Nawahī, a noted 19th-century Hawaiian leader. Nawahī, who was born in Kaimū, Puna, in 1854, was reared by the Reverend David B. Lyman and educated at the Lahainaluna Seminary. He and his wife, Aima, started and edited the newspaper *Ke Aloha 'Āina*, dedicated to the sovereignty of Hawai'i. Nawahī also painted in oil, and a few of his paintings survive. *C.J. Hedemann Collection*

57 Shipman House

W.H. Shipman bought this Victorian mansion, just a couple years old here in 1901, as a surprise for his wife, Mary, and their children. He was a cattle rancher and son of missionaries; Mary was a Hawaiian of high rank, her grandfather one of the first white men to stay in Hawai'i. Jack London was once a month-long guest here, and Queen Lili'uokalani was a friend who came to luncheon and played the grand piano that still sits in the parlor. Shipman House is now a bed-and-breakfast operation run by the couple's great-granddaughter and her husband. *Shipman House Collection*

"To charm the eye..."

The bay of Hilo is a beautiful, spacious and safe harbor. The outline of its beach is a crescent like the moon in her first quarter. The beach is composed of fine, volcanic sand, mixed with a little coral and earth. On its eastern and western sides, and in its center, it is divided by three streams of pure water; it has a deep channel about half a mile wide, near the western shore, sufficiently deep to admit the largest ship that floats. Seaward it is protected by a lava reef one mile from the shore. This reef was formed by a lateral stream of lava, sent out at right angles from a broad river of molten rocks that formed our eastern coast. This reef is a grand barrier against the swell of the ocean. Lord Byron, who visited Hilo, when he brought home the corpses of King Liholiho and his queen, gave the name of 'Byron's Bay' to this harbor, but that name is nearly obsolete....

The beach was once beautifully adorned with the cocoa palm, whose lofty plumes waved and rustled and glittered in the fresh sea-breeze. Beyond our quiet bay the broad, blue ocean foams or sleeps, with a surface sometimes shining like molten silver, tumbling in white foam, or gently throbbing as with the pulsations of life....

Inland, from the shore to the bases of the mountains, the whole landscape is 'arrayed in living green,' presenting a picture of inimitable beauty, so varied in tint, so grooved with water channels, and so sparkling with limpid streams and white foaming cascades, as to charm the eye, and cause the beholder to exclaim, 'This is a scene of surpassing loveliness.'...We were satisfied, yes more, we were delighted, with our location, and to this day we bless the Lord that He inclined the minds of the mission to assign us to this field of labor.

– *Titus Coan,* Life In Hawaii, *1882*

65 Lyman Mission House

The New England-style home erected by Christian missionaries David and Sarah Lyman in 1839 still stands on Haili Street. The oldest frame building on the island, it's now a museum, furnished as though the Lyman family were in residence. Over the years many guests, including all the monarchs from Kamehameha III to Lili'uokalani as well as foreign visitors such as Mark Twain, stayed with the Lymans. The mission house opened as a museum in 1931, and in 1971 a two-story museum building was built next door. *Lyman Museum*

"Called to say aroha..."

July 17, 1832. A kind Providence has protected us and led us on our way when dangers have stood thick around, and have brought us after 8 long months of wandering to the field where we trust it is His will we should labour… Arrived here in safety last evening…. A great many people called to say aroha to us, among the rest was an interesting little girl, the daughter of one of the chiefs. She was dressed in a calico slip with a wreath of yellow flowers around her head and neck. She approached and gave me her hand with as good grace as any little girl in America. After giving the customary salutation she seated herself on the mat near to where I sat.

– *From* The Lymans of Hilo, *a journal kept by missionary Sarah Joiner Lyman*

61 Boiling Pots

Boiling Pots is a beautiful site in the Wailuku River where water travels between successive pools through underground lava tubes. It appears to "boil" as it funnels out of one "pot" and then appears in the next pool downstream. According to legend, the god Maui was avenging an injury against his mother, Hina, one day when he chased the monstrous Kuna into a deep pool of the Wailuku River. Maui called upon the volcano goddess Pele to send hot rocks and lava, which caused the waters to boil furiously. Time, says the legend, has cooled the waters, but they continue to bubble as though boiling.

C.J. Hedemann Collection

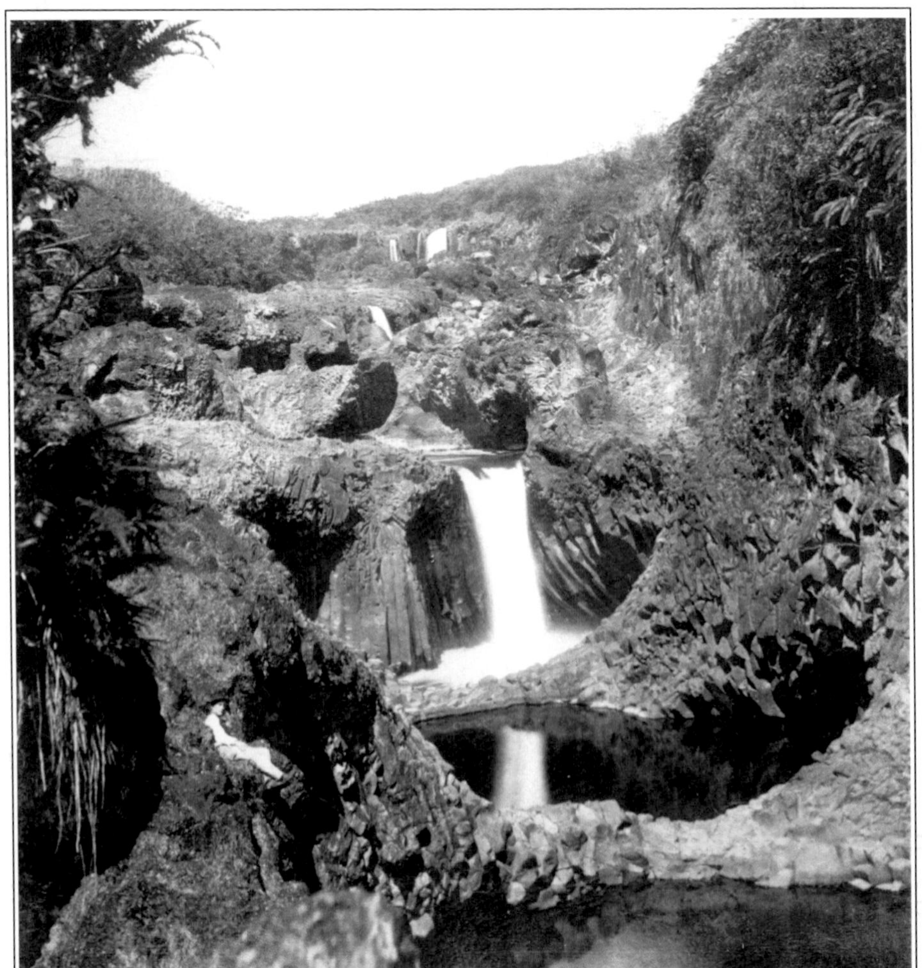

Chapter Eight

Hilo Memories

56 Naha and Pinao Stones

Most Big Island historians believe that the Naha and Pinao stones were brought from Kaua'i in ancient times and placed in front of Pinao Heiau, formerly located between the present Methodist Church and the Hawai'i State Library parking lot. In 1916 the stones were moved to a public library site on Keawe Street. In 1951, they were placed in front of the Waiānuenue Avenue public library, close to the former heiau site, where they remain. The Naha stone was historically significant in ceremonies for the birth of a Naha chief. Its most famous association is the fulfilled prophecy that Kamehameha would conquer the islands if he was able to move the massive stone, which he did. *Bishop Museum*

5 Hilo Yacht Club

The Hilo Yacht Club was launched when a group of Hilo men met in 1913 to form a social club "to promote aquatic and other athletic sports and pastimes." The club's first location, here on Reed's Bay where the Naniloa Hotel currently stands, was the C.C. Kennedy beach house. In 1920 a new clubhouse was built on the bay off Banyan Drive. In 1937 the club moved to the former Harlocker home at Keaukaha. The 1946 tsunami obliterated those buildings, but the club was rebuilt. Today the membership club offers fine dining, tennis, a black sand volleyball court and an ocean-view pool. *Ian Birnie Collection*

"Forced to land in the forest"

The first seaplane to attempt to land in Hilo Bay was a Curtiss R-6 Army Air Corp plane piloted by Maj. Harold Clark and Sgt. Robert Gray that came from Kahului Harbor in 1918 delivering mail to Hilo.

Clark got lost in dense clouds above the Kaiwiki area, clipped a few trees and was forced to land in the forest above the sugar fields. The two Army pilots walked for two days before they were found in Kaiwiki and taken to Hilo.

The first successful landing in Hilo Bay was when Maj. Hugh Kneer landed in Hilo Bay in a U.S. Army A-1816 hydroplane on a flight from Honolulu in May 1919.

– *From* Big Island's Moms & Pops, Before Wal-Marts and K-Marts, *by Wayne A. Subica, Memories of Hawaii, 2006*

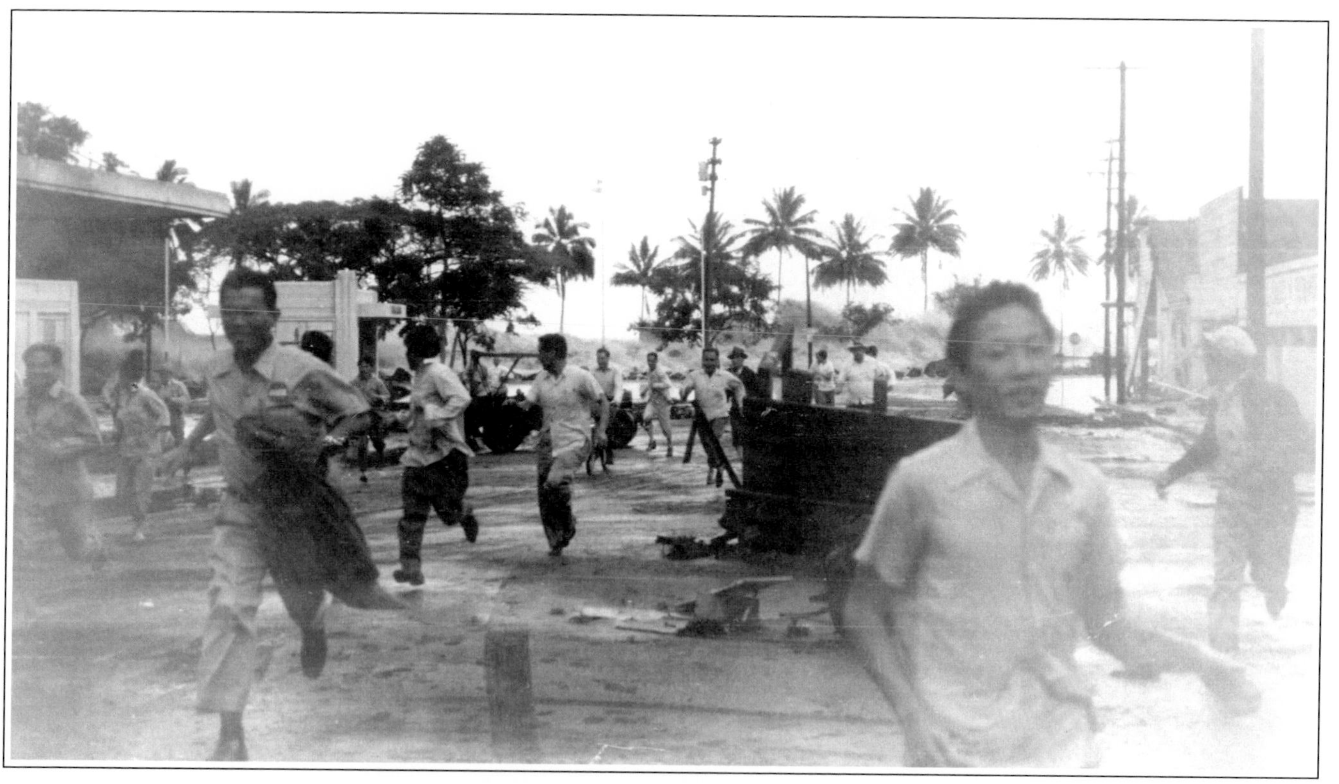

17 Ponahawai Street and Kamehameha Avenue

This often-published photo shows crowds running from the third of nine tsunami waves to hit downtown Hilo on the morning of April 1, 1946. The photo was taken from Ruddle Sales and Service on the corner of Ponahawai Street and Kamehameha Avenue, and shows people running up Ponahawai Street. As the waves pass through Moʻoheau Park in the background they are as tall as some of the coconut trees. The highest waves were 55 feet, with an average along Hilo Bay of 30 feet. *Cecilio Licos/Eugene Koya Collection/Pacific Tsunami Museum*

"A scramble among rocks and holes..."

Miss Karpe, my travelling companion, is a lady of great energy, and adept in the art of travelling. Undismayed by three days of sea-sickness, and the prospect of the tremendous journey to the volcano tomorrow, she extemporised a ride to the Anuenue [Rainbow] Falls on the Wailuku this afternoon, and I weakly accompanied her, a burly policeman being our guide. The track is only a scramble among rocks and holes, concealed by grass and ferns, and we had to cross a stream, full of great holes, several times. The Fall itself is very pretty, 110 feet in one descent, with a cavernous shrine behind the water, filled with ferns. There were large ferns all round the Fall, and a jungle of luxuriant tropical shrubs of many kinds.

– *Isabella Bird,* Six Months in the Sandwich Islands, *1873*

62 Rainbow Falls

Until 1892, the scenic spot up Waiānuenue Avenue now called Rainbow Falls, formerly Ānuenue Falls, was accessible only by horse trail. In 1904 the Hilo Park Commission widened the trail to accommodate carriages and it started landscaping. A favorite sport in earlier times was "lele kawa," or leaping from a height into the water; and 30- to 40-foot leaps were made at Rainbow Falls. *C.J. Hedemann Collection*

28 Parade Downtown, ca. 1915

This is likely an early Independence Day parade, traveling down Kamehameha Avenue toward King Street (now Kalākaua Street) where the power pole stands. Note the American flags on the early carriages, the pā‘ū riders and the crowd's natty attire. The second-floor verandah at the center of the photo was the site of the old consulate office, standing where Basically Books is located today. Because wooden buildings don't last long in Hawai‘i's tropical weather, many of these buildings no longer exist and others now stand in their place.
Koehnen's Collection

"Eight girls from Hilo..."

On Monday, the 25th, the thermometer stood at 20 deg. at sunrise. Messrs. Muir and Alexander ascended the second highest peak on the northwest, overlooking Waimea, 13,645 feet height to continue their survey. In the cairn on the summit a tin can was found that contains brief records of the visits of five different parties from 1870 to the present time, to which we added our own. A party of eight girls from Hilo, "personally conducted" by Dr. Wetmore and D.H. Hitchcock, Esq, in 1876, must have been a merry one. Cpt. Long of H.B.M.'s Ship Fantome had visited this spot in 1876, and Dr. Arning with several Kohala residents in 1885.

– *W.D. Alexander,* Hawaiian Gazette, *1892*

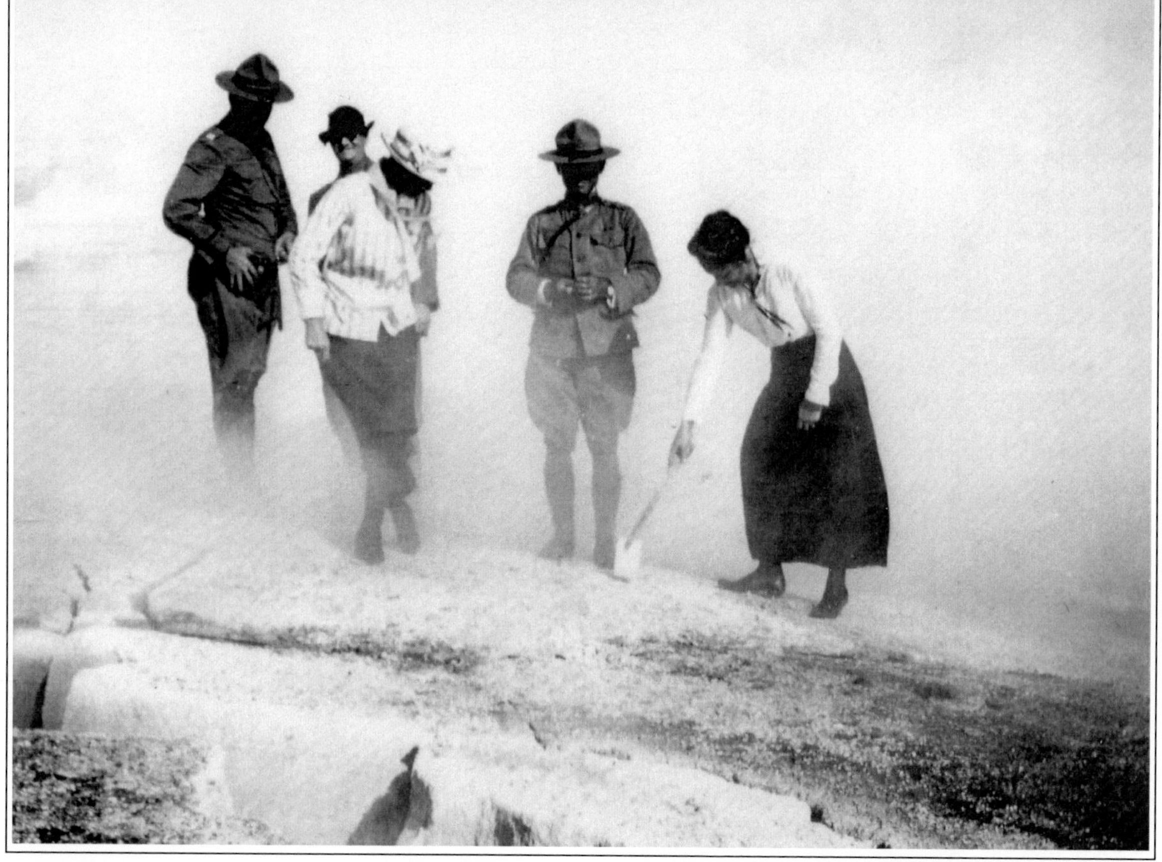

78 Kīlauea Caldera

Hilo has long served as the gateway to Kīlauea, the active volcano that today is the heart of Hawai'i Volcanoes National Park. Established in 1916, the 217,000-acre park now encompasses the summit and forests of Mauna Loa, the Ka'u Desert and the rugged coastal stretch of the Puna/Ka'u Historic District. Here, inside Kīlauea Caldera, sightseers scorch postcards in hot lava, to be mailed home as dramatic proof of their visit. Hawai'i Volcanoes National Park was named a UNESCO World Heritage Site in 1987. *Hawai'i State Archives*

44 Palm Tree

For decades, a palm tree growing in the middle of Kamehameha Avenue, near Waiānuenue Avenue, marked the heights of various tsunamis that had hit the town. A ship's spike was driven through the tree's trunk at 25 feet, for instance, to mark the height of the 1868 tsunami. Eventually the landmark tree was even protected by county ordinance. In 1910, a permit was issued allowing workers to bend the tree while moving the first Hackfeld Company building across the street to its new, makai, location. During that operation, the tree broke.

Koehnen's Collection

Resources

Bird, Isabella L., *Six Months in the Sandwich Islands*. Honolulu: Mutual Publishing, 1998. First printed in 1881 by G.P. Putnam's Sons, New York.

Coan, Titus, *Life in Hawaii, an Autobiographic Sketch of Mission Life and Labors (1835-1882)*. New York: Anson D. F. Randolph & Company, 1882.

Downtown Hilo Walking Tour of Historic Downtown (Hilo Downtown Improvement Association, et al.)

Dudley, Walt and Stone, Scott C.S., *The Tsunami of 1946 and 1960 and the Devastation of Hilo Town*. Virginia Beach, VA: Donning Co., 2000.

George, Milton C., *The Development of Hilo, Hawaii, T.H. A Modern Tropical Sugar Port*. 1948.

Haili Church, 150 Years, 1974

Hawaii Tribune-Herald

Hilo, A Walking Tour of Historic and Cultural Sites, American Assoc. of University Women and Lyman House Memorial Museum, 1996.

Hilo March: Guided Tour Through Historic Hilo. AAUW, Hilo Branch

Hilo Tribune-Herald

Alvarez, Patricia M., *History of Road and Bridge Development on the Island of Hawaii*. Hawaiian State Dept of Transportation, 1985.

Honolulu Advertiser

Honolulu Star-Bulletin

Hungerford, John B., *Hawaiian Railroads*.

Kelly, Marion, Nakamura, Barry and Barrere, Dorothy A., *Hilo Bay, A Chronological History, Land and Water Use in the Hilo Bay Area, Island of Hawaii*. Department of Anthropology, Bernice P. Bishop Museum. Prepared for the U.S. Army Engineer District, Honolulu, March 1981.

Lydgate, J. M., "Hilo Fifty Years Ago." *Thrum's Hawaiian Annual*, 1923.

Lyman House Memorial Museum, *The Lymans of Hilo*, Hilo, 1992.

Paradise of the Pacific magazine, Honolulu

References to the Naha and Pinao Stones: A Chronological and Annotated Bibliography. Hawaii Department of Land and Natural Resources, 1997.

Smith, Charlotte Hapai, *Hilo Legends*. Hilo: Petroglyph Press, Ltd., 1966.

Subica, Wayne A., *Big Island's Moms & Pops, Before Wal-Marts & K-Marts*. Hilo: Memories of Hawaii, 2006.

Subica, Wayne A., *Hilo High School – "First" 100 Years*. Memories of Hawaii, 2006.

Takaki, Ronald, *Pau Hana, Plantation Life and Labor in Hawaii, 1835-1920, Hawaii*. Honolulu: University of Hawaii Press, 1983.

Index

122